A CHANGED MAN

NANCY SUNDQUIST

GLOBE FEARON
Pearson Learning Group

The PACEMAKER BESTELLERS

Bestellers I

Diamonds in the Dirt
Night of the Kachina
The Verlaine Crossing
Silvabamba
The Money Game

Flight to Fear
The Time Trap
The Candy Man
Three Mile House
Dream of the Dead

Bestellers II

Black Beach
Crash Dive
Wind Over Stonehenge
Gypsy
Escape from Tomorrow

The Demeter Star
North to Oak Island
So Wild a Dream
Wet Fire
Tiger, Lion, Hawk

Bestellers III

Star Gold
Bad Moon
Jungle Jenny
Secret Spy
Little Big Top

The Animals
Counterfeit!
Night of Fire and Blood
Village of Vampires
I Died Here

Bestellers IV

Dares
Welcome to Skull Canyon
Blackbeard's Medal
Time's Reach
Trouble at Catskill Creek

The Cardiff Hill Mystery
Tomorrow's Child
Hong Kong Heat
Follow the Whales
A Changed Man

Cover and interior illustrator: JamesMcConnell

ISBN 0-8224-5344-4   Printed in the United States of America

5 6 7 8 9 10 11   05 04 03 02

1-800-321-3106
www.pearsonlearning.com

CONTENTS

CHAPTER 1

ALL AT ONCE

I was driving my dad's new DeSoto to a 10:00 A.M. class at UCLA. The news from Europe had just come over the radio. The Allies had taken Paris. "As Time Goes By" began to play, and I sang along. The early morning air smelled clean. The road ahead was empty. We were winning the war. I felt great.

I turned north on Sepulveda and stepped on the gas. The Santa Monica Mountains were miles away, but I could see them clearly. After Wilshire Boulevard, I passed the Veterans Cemetery. It made me think of all the lives the war was costing us. I felt bad about not being able to go off and fight. Two years earlier, I'd tried to enlist. But the army wouldn't take me because of my flat feet.

Suddenly, I spotted something up the road. A beat-up Ford had pulled over to the side. Standing next to it was a beautiful young woman who was waving her arms. She had long red hair and was wearing a blue dress. I looked more closely and saw that her car had a flat. I slowed down to stop and help her, and that's when it happened. That's when my life turned inside out.

All at once, the road is as wide as a football field. There are cars all around me. They're moving so fast they seem to be flying. And they're so small they look like toys. They're strange colors, too. Bright greens and oranges and colors I've never seen on cars are flashing by.

The Santa Monica Mountains are still in sight. Yet I can hardly see them because the air is thick with yellow dust. I look at the road before me. It's way too close. I'm in a car that's half the size of Dad's DeSoto. The controls look like those on a spaceship.

A wide belt across my body is pressing me against the seat. The windows are up, but ice cold air is blowing on my legs. Strange loud music is coming at me from all sides. I look for the radio. It's then that I catch sight of the face in the mirror. The face is my own, but it's aged many years. I lift my hands from the wheel to touch my face. Suddenly the car starts to spin.

CHAPTER 2

YOU DON'T UNDERSTAND!

I wake up on a table in what looks like a hospital. I'm off in the corner of a large room. Several yards away is a long desk. Three nurses sit behind it looking busy. The wall clock above them says eight o'clock. My guess is that I've been lying there all day.

People in white are rushing in and out of the room. I hear a man close by screaming, "My leg, my leg!" A voice on the P.A. keeps saying, "Dr. Gordon, you're wanted at the front desk. Dr. Gordon . . ." I try to sit up, but my head is hurting. I lie back down. A nurse comes over and says, "You're lucky. You made it through the crash, but your car didn't. We wanted to call your family, but you're not carrying your driver's license."

"Dad's car . . ." I say.

"The car was all smashed up. Was it new?"

"As new as they come these days, what with the war on and all. About a month ago, Dad found a good buy on a new DeSoto. He's going to kill me."

The nurse is looking at me kind of funny, but I go on talking. "All of a sudden, I just couldn't control the car. I was on Sepulveda and . . ."

"That's strange," the nurse says. "Our records show they picked you up going north on the San Diego Freeway."

"Freeway?" I say. "San Diego?"

"Listen," the nurse says, getting down to business. "We need to know some things about you." She pulls a pen from her pocket. "First, can you tell me your name?"

"Sam Smith," I answer.

"Who's your insurance with, Sam?"

"I don't know, really. My dad's company covers me."

Again, the nurse looks at me funny. "Could you give me your father's telephone number?"

"It's Crestview-two-two-three-hundred."

"You mean 'two-seven-two-two-three-hundred?'"

"Whatever," I say. I am suddenly tired of all her questions. She asks a few more of them

and then walks away. The man with the hurt leg has stopped screaming. I close my eyes and think back to the crash. It seems like a bad dream. First I was in a DeSoto and then in a who-knows-what? Maybe I've been up too many nights studying. Maybe I've lost my mind. Suddenly, I hear a voice.

"Hello, Mr. Smith. I'm Dr. Gordon. I'd like to ask you a few questions. First of all, are you seeing okay?"

"I think so," I answer. The doctor shines a light in one eye and then the other.

"How many fingers do you see?" he asks, holding up his first two fingers.

"Two," I say.

The doctor shines his light in my ears and looks into my mouth.

"Do you know what country you're in?"

"The United States," I say, thinking he's probably checking for brain damage.

"How about the president of the United States?"

"Roosevelt."

Dr. Gordon takes a long hard look at me. He asks a few more questions. Then he walks away. The nurse returns and says I gave her a wrong number. She asks for someone else in the family. I explain I'm an only child. She asks for a friend's or a neighbor's number. I give her two. She comes back with the same story. Both were wrong numbers. Before I can say anything, she's called away.

Slowly I sit up and rub my head. My hands are shaking. With no one around, I look at myself for the first time since the crash. I'm still in street clothes because the doctor hasn't given me a room yet. But I'm wearing a coat and tie that I've never seen before. I spot a mirror on the wall next to me. I think about looking in it. But I'm afraid of what I'll see. The face I saw in the car mirror flashes across my mind. I force myself to look.

I face the mirror and see an old man.

When Dr. Gordon returns, I'm beside myself with worry. "Look, Doctor," I say, "you've got to help me. I'm not this old. Something has happened to me."

"Now, now, Mr. Smith," he says, "take it easy, take it easy. You've been knocked around a bit. I'm not surprised you're forgetting a few things. In time—"

I cut him off, shouting, "You don't understand! This is not a question of forgetting a few years. I'm a young man. I'm a student at UCLA, in the class of '45. . . . I was late. . . . It was morning. . . . I was in my dad's car, on Sepulveda—"

"Mr. Smith, stop. Before you go on, let me say something. We would like to help you. It's just that we can only take people with insurance. Now, we've called General Hospital, and you're in luck. They have a few beds free—"

"Not General!" I shout. "People don't get good care there."

"General has fine doctors. You'll be in good hands. They'll run tests on you right away. Really now, there's no cause for worry."

"Thank you, doctor," I say. What I'm thinking, however, is that I've *got* to get out of there!

"I'll see if I can get your papers ready. Don't worry about a ride. Someone who works here will drive you over."

Dr. Gordon leaves my side. Slowly I get to my feet. The room spins. A few nurses and doctors are still racing around. No one is watching me. I carefully put one foot in front of the other. Soon I'm walking past the front desk. My hand is on the door when a nurse stops me.

"Oh," I say, trying to hide my fear that she won't let me leave. "Didn't Dr. Gordon tell you? I'm going over to General. My ride is waiting."

"Very well, Mr. Smith," the nurse says with a smile. "Good luck to you."

I push open the door—and see sunlight! I've been thinking it was evening. Now I understand that I must have been in the hospital all night long. I reach into my pocket and pull out some money and a broken cigarette. I don't know what the cigarette is doing there. I throw it away and count my money. I've got a few dollars and some change. I'm in good shape, I think. I start down the steps. The same toy cars I saw before the crash line the street. They shine in the morning sunlight. Either I'm in a strange place or a different time, I don't know which. I feel like I'm floating through the air. A young woman about my age comes walking toward me. She has short green hair that's sticking out all over. She's dressed in black baggy shorts, a yellow undershirt, and red shoes. I walk up to her and say, "Hello, there. Would you mind telling me what part of town this is?"

This woman looks at me like I'm the one who's strange. "Westwood," she says.

"Westwood?"

"You got it, Pops," she says before walking on.

Suddenly I remember that I look three times as old as I feel. And who knows? Maybe I *am* the strange one. I decide I'd better think twice before speaking.

I walk a few blocks. The streets are empty. I look in shop windows. In one, I see UCLA T-shirts and UCLA coffee cups and UCLA pens.

Businesses of all kinds line Westwood Boulevard. As many as three different movie houses are in sight. I look south, to where I remember Wilshire Boulevard should be. A few blocks down, giant buildings almost block out the sky.

I decide to catch a bus for home. I walk to Wilshire and find a bus stop and a place to sit. By now it's clear that many years have passed, for the city as well as for me.

CHAPTER 3

THE HOUSE MY FATHER BUILT

The sun is hardly up, and already it's hot. I'm sitting at the bus stop, not even knowing what day it is. From time to time, I look down the street for the yellow and gray L.A. Motor Coach. Suddenly, the largest thing I've ever seen on wheels is coming around the corner. Its dark windows keep me from seeing inside. When it stops its doors swing open.

"Coming or going?" the driver asks.

I can hardly speak. "Is this the bus? . . ."

"You might call it that. Come on, mister, I don't have all day."

I climb the steps and hand the driver seven cents.

"Sorry, mister, the ride will cost you eighty-five cents."

"Eighty-five cents!" I shout. "I can almost fill my car up for eighty-five cents!"

"I'd sure like to know where you buy your gas," the driver says. Then he points to the clear box next to him and says, "Eighty-five cents. Or get off the bus."

I throw in the money and take a seat up front. On the floor is the morning's *Los Angeles Times*. I pick it up and read the day's date: Saturday, August 30, 1986.

That makes me 62 years old.

"Did we win the war?" I ask, bending toward the driver.

"Which war might that be, mister?"

"The war with Hitler."

"Oh, that one. Yes, we won that one some time ago." He looks up at me through the big mirror over his head.

I know he's wondering if I'm in my right mind. I decide not to ask any more questions. Finally, I get off in Cheviot Hills, a small pocket of homes in West L.A. I walk the few blocks to my house. I'm thinking hard. *If I'm this old, my parents will be in their 80s.* Still, against all reason, I'm hoping to go home and find that nothing has changed. Mom will be in the kitchen making breakfast. Dad will be in the backyard reading the paper. I'm hoping it really was his DeSoto I crashed. I'm hoping I'm just a kid who's gotten into a little trouble with his dad's new car. I also know I'm hoping against hope.

At the top of the hill, I stop dead. At the bottom of the block, where the woods used to be, there's now a river of cars. The woods I used to play in is simply no longer there.

Then it hits me. In the crash, I was on a highway like this one. All of a sudden, it *wasn't* Sepulveda anymore. What had the nurse called it—the San Diego Freeway? Were there more than one of these freeways in Los Angeles? The highway I was looking at now went east and west. The highway I'd crashed on went north and south. But why was it called the San Diego Freeway? Could it be that it went all the way to San Diego?

The only highway I know of that's more than two lanes wide is the Arroyo Seco Parkway. It was the first highway of its kind in Los Angeles—in the country, for that matter. I remember when it opened, only four years ago. Or I guess I should say 46 years ago. The mayor had cut the ribbon only three days earlier. My dad and I drove on the new road. We were going to the Rose Bowl. And so was everyone in town! Dad and I had a good laugh. The Arroyo Parkway was supposed to be the answer to traffic jams. Well, Dad and I sat in the biggest traffic jam we'd ever seen. So much for city planning!

Suddenly, a hand grabs my arm from behind. I turn and see Pete, our gardener. He was just a boy when I saw him last. He's now an old man.

"Sam Smith," he says. "It's been years since I've seen you."

"It has been a long time," I answer.

"The place sure has changed since you lived here, hasn't it? After your parents died in that plane crash . . . well, things have just never been the same."

A heavy sadness washes over me. It's all I can do to stay standing. *My parents? Dead?*

Pete talks on. "These days I don't bother getting to know the new people. They move in and out so fast. I just do my job. . . . So what have you been up to Sam? What have you done with your life?"

"Oh, keeping busy. I just thought I'd stop by and see the old place."

"Sure, you do that, Sam. And don't be such a stranger anymore, you hear?"

"I won't, Pete. Not if I can help it. It's nice seeing you again."

I watch Pete climb slowly into his truck full of yard tools. Then I walk toward the house I grew up in.

A young woman opens the front door. I explain that my parents built the house in the early 30s. "Would you mind," I ask, "if I take a quick look around?"

"Of course not," she answers as she leads me into the dining room. "I'm glad you came by.

My husband and I ran across a box of someone's belongings a while back. We had just moved in and found it in one of the back rooms. The owners before us said it wasn't theirs. It's a good thing I didn't throw it away. Let me go get it."

She leaves, and I look around. I can still hear the cars racing by outside. Yesterday flowered paper covered the dining room walls. Today they're painted a light gray. Yesterday our old Philco radio took up a whole corner. Today a large box with a square of green glass on the front of it sits in its place. I feel lost and mixed-up. I step to the window that once overlooked the woods and watch the cars streaming by.

"The Santa Monica wasn't built yet when you lived here, was it?"

I turn and see the woman in the doorway behind me. She's holding an old Sunkist Oranges box. "No," I say. "It was more peaceful then."

"I just tell myself the ocean's making all that noise," she says. She sets the box down on the dining room table. I smile, thinking she's got a point. The cars do make a sound like the waves at the beach.

"Take your time going through it. I'll be in the kitchen. Can I get you anything to eat or drink?"

"No, thank you." Food is the last thing on my mind. I sit at the table and lift off the top of the box. A rolled sheet of paper lies to one side. I open it up. Printed at the top, in a child's hand are the words "California Wild Flowers." In the bottom right corner is the name Sam Smith. Bright yellow and pink dots float in a sea of green.

I lift out a book with "UCLA, 1945" on its cover. I find my name in the list of students in the back of the book. I turn to page 385. There I am, one year older than I remember myself being. In the picture, I'm smiling as if nothing were wrong. The picture should belong to my future, not my past. Standing next to me is my friend Hugh Hammill, the smartest person I know. We both are—or both *were*—students in the business school.

Sticking between the pages is a picture of me and another friend, Brad Amis. It was taken when Brad was home on leave from the war. We're standing next to the DeSoto. Our arms are around each other.

The other things are mostly from my early years, probably saved by Mom. Still, they're all I have. My whole life is held in this box. I laugh dryly as I lift out a watch. On its back are the words "To Sam, at 16, Love Dad." I put it on and then check the time on the grandfather's clock behind me. It says ten o'clock.

It's ten o'clock, Saturday morning, August 30, 1986. My parents are dead. I'm 62. My body—and the world—are 42 years older.

I've got some catching up to do.

Setting my watch, I thank the woman and say I'll be back for the box. I leave the house, hoping that nothing does stop me from returning. That's how out of control I feel.

CHAPTER 4

FRIENDLY LITTLE VISITS

I walk back down the street I grew up on, trying to put the puzzle together. So many of its pieces seem to be missing.

The yearbook showed me that my life didn't end in 1944. But I know nothing about that life. Do I have a family, a wife and children, a home of my own? What have I been doing all these years?

I find myself hoping I have amnesia. Then at least I'd know what was wrong with me. But of course that wouldn't answer all my questions. Where was my family when I was in the hospital? Might they be looking for me now? Where was my driver's license? Why do I remember nothing of my life after 1944? Why do I remember my life up to 1944 so clearly?

I decide to walk over to the Palms Public Library. There I can read up on the missing years. I can even check the phone books and maybe find out where I live now. Seeing my home might help me remember things. I walk south on Motor Avenue and turn left on Woodbine.

There is a small playground where the library once stood.

I walk back to Motor and head south, toward some shops. On my right, I spot a building with a sign saying AM/PM Mini Mart. Outside is a kind of phone stand. I open the phone book tied to it and find the Smiths. A full page of S. Smiths and Sam Smiths swims before my eyes. I carefully read the street name next to each one. None of them feels like home.

Then I get the idea to look up Brad. There aren't many Amises, and I find only one Brad, in West Hollywood. I decide to drop by instead of calling. "If anyone can help me, it's Brad," I say out loud.

I catch a bus headed north, up Motor Avenue. The driver is a woman! I ask her if the bus goes to West Hollywood. She tells me she can drop me off south of West Hollywood. There, she says, for ten cents more I can catch another bus going north. I pay the woman, she

hands me a ticket, and I take a seat. At the end of Motor, the bus stops at a red light. Before us is 20th Century Fox. I shouldn't be surprised that this giant movie-maker is still around. Yet by this time I am.

The light turns—not just to green, but to a green arrow. Not even the traffic lights have stayed the same. The bus jumps forward and swings east on Pico Boulevard. At La Cienega, I change to another bus. Looking out the window, I can't believe how the city has changed. There's so much more traffic and noise. We pass buildings being torn down and buildings being put up. Everywhere I look the city seems to be growing. Then there are the people. To me they seem to be strange beings of the future. They dress differently, talk differently, even move differently. And everyone seems to be in such a rush! After a couple of miles, I get out and walk over to Alfred Street.

I stop in front of Brad's house, thinking about what I'll say. I spot an older man alongside the house. He's sitting on the ground, digging in a vegetable garden. The man is heavyset, with graying hair. Suddenly I realize he's Brad. Without thinking, I'd planned on him looking like he did at 20. I stand there for a minute or two without speaking. I try to remember something—*anything*—that has happened to me since 1944.

Suddenly, Brad sees me and shouts, "What on earth do you think you're doing here? This is my land. I want you off it right now. Hear me? Off!"

I don't know what to say. Finally I say, "Brad, it's me, Sam! What's the problem?"

"As if you didn't know! Maybe it's just that little Catalina house we went in on together. Maybe I can't forget how you rented it out without telling me. Maybe I can't forget all that money you were pocketing. You really take the cake, Sam. . . . Coming to pay me a friendly little visit after all the things you've done to me."

"Brad, *wait* a minute! I don't know what you're talking about."

This couldn't be going worse, I say to myself. Here I was so happy to have found someone I knew. To see that he hates me is more than I can bear.

"Oh, come on, Sam, cut the act. You may want to forget all the people you've robbed. But I'm here to tell you something. I'll *never* let you forget—not for as long as I live!"

If only he knew how much I wished he could do just that. "Brad," I say, "you've got to believe me. I don't remember anything after 1944. I need help. I came here thinking of you as a friend. I—"

"I'm sorry, Sam. 'Friend' is a word for what you used to be." Brad walks into his house. The door slams shut behind him.

With my hands in my pockets, I turn and head back toward La Cienega. At the corner there's a gas station and another outdoor phone. Maybe Hugh Hammill can fill me in on what went wrong between Brad and me. I'm not surprised to find Hugh listed in Beverly Hills. I feel sure he's made a big name for himself. I check my money and see I have enough for just one more bus ride. Looking for the nearest stop, I catch a big sign posting the cost of gas. It reads 99 cents. *How do people get by?* I wonder.

Standing at Hugh's door, I first hear a woman laughing and then music. *Someone's listening to a radio show*, I think. I knock, and Hugh himself opens the door. Behind him is a wooden box much like the one I saw at my old house. Only this one has a moving picture behind the glass. The picture is even in color! A young woman and man are playing around in the ocean waves. Suddenly, the woman jumps out of the water onto the sand.

"What do *you* want?" Hugh says.

I can't take my eyes off the movie. The woman is wearing almost nothing! Is this the television experiment I read about at school? Most people thought it would never take the place of radio. But a few people had said there'd soon be one in every home.

"What do you want?" Hugh asks again.

I tear my eyes from the movie and look up at Hugh. He's still tall, but is, of course, much older. He looks like he hasn't slept in days. There are deep circles under his eyes. His gray hair is thinning and his mouth is lined with worry.

"Hugh!" I say, happy to see him and hoping he's okay.

He doesn't smile. He doesn't ask me in. He just stands there, with anger in his eyes.

"Hugh, I'm sorry for breaking in on you like this. I'm in a little trouble. I was thinking maybe you could help me."

"Help you? Help *you*? Like you helped me?"

"What do you mean?"

"You don't remember a year ago? You've forgotten when I came to you without a cent to my name?" Hugh is starting to shout.

"Hugh, I've forgotten a lot since—"

"There you are, President of North American Testing. You have hundreds of people working for you. You have enough money to redo all your offices in Century City—"

"Hugh, you've got to listen to me," I say, but Hugh is too busy talking.

I look over Hugh's shoulder into his living room. Anyone could see that Hugh hasn't done well. The chairs are worn. The walls need paint. The wood floors need sanding.

Yet Hugh does have a television. Now the woman and man are lying on the sand. Their bodies are very close. The music is getting louder. Suddenly, the picture changes from a beach to a house. Another woman—fully clothed—stands next to a washing machine. She's smiling and holding a box of soap.

"And there I am," Hugh is saying. "Down on my luck, a man who can't pay his next month's rent. Sam, I could hardly pay for a *bus ride* to Century Park East. It took a lot out of me to ask you for a job. You know I'm not the kind to ask for handouts. But that's what you made me feel like I was doing. I left your office feeling about as low as a man can feel. But then I realized something, Sam. I realized I hadn't come down as low as you had."

"Hugh, I'm sorry. You've got to believe me. I am truly sorry for any hurt I've caused you."

Hugh fixes his eyes on the floor. I turn to leave and say, "I'll try to make it up to you, Hugh."

I walk away from Hugh's house, feeling worse than ever.

How could I have turned on my best friends? I hadn't given Hugh work when he needed it. And to hear Brad tell it, I'd robbed him of house and home. All of it is more than I can understand.

What I do know now is that I work in Century City. It's a place I've never even heard of.

CHAPTER 5

SOMETHING CAME UP

I walk to Rodeo Drive and stop to get my bearings. It's only four o'clock. But I feel like I haven't slept in days. For all I know, I haven't. Then again, maybe I'm just feeling like the old man I seem to have become.

I'm south of Wilshire now, west of La Cienega. I spot a man getting out of a parked car. I decide to take the chance and ask what's probably another silly question. "Hello, there," I say, trying to sound friendly. "I'm new in town and . . . well, could you tell me where Century City is?"

My cover works. The man simply says, "Follow Rodeo to Olympic and hang a right."

Hang is a word I guess to mean "turn." It's hard getting used to the way people talk.

"What street are you looking for?" the man asks.

What was that street Hugh said he could hardly pay for a bus ride to? At the time he said it, I was thinking of how much money I had left. The 43 cents in my pocket was enough to take me nowhere. Finally, it comes to me. "Century Park East," I say, pleased my memory hasn't gone all together.

"It'll be the first street. Century City is less than a mile down Olympic."

"Thanks for the help." I walk away glad to have been able to speak to someone without feeling strange.

By this time, my feet are killing me. But nothing—not even flat feet—can stop me from going on. I turn my thoughts to my job. Hugh made it sound like I'd done pretty well for myself.

So I have my own company, do I? North American Testing . . . I wonder what it is.

I reach Olympic and head west. I'm thinking that 20th Century Fox's back lot should be about a mile down Olympic. That's where Fox shoots many of its movies. What could have happened to it?

A few blocks later, the sight of tall glass buildings stops me in my tracks. As I feared, Fox's back lot is now Century City. I remember the Fox movies I've enjoyed, like *Guns Along the Mohawk*, and *Grapes of Wrath*. Many of them were made where these glass buildings now stand.

On Century Park East, I walk into the closest building. On a wall inside the front doors is a listing of all the companies in the building. North American Testing is not one of them. I check a few more buildings. Finally, I find one that has a North American Testing Services on its 30th floor. There are three banks of elevators. I find one that says 21–30 and press "UP." The doors open, but the elevator is empty. I step inside, and press "30."

I feel myself going up. Seconds later, the doors open. I'm now looking at a room right out of the space age. It's been done in blacks and grays and deep reds. Before me is a black desk shaped in a half-circle. Behind it is a large open space with maybe 30 other desks. Offices line three walls. Their doors are open. I can see that they look out over the city.

I recognize nothing.

I walk into the room and stop by one of the desks. On it is a pile of paper, maybe 200 sheets. The first page reads, "Happiness in Marriage." On the second page, there are some 15 questions. The first is, "My husband/wife is my best friend." To the right are boxes for checking off Yes or No. I turn the pages and see hundreds of questions like this one.

I stop at another desk. Sitting on top of the typewriter is a glass square. "A television at work?" I ask out loud. Then I see a sheet of paper several feet long with holes on its sides. It lists hundreds of tests, like "Your Baby's IQ" and "Finding the Right Job." Next to each are the sales figures for the last year. I spot a test called "How Good Is Your Memory?" I'm thinking about taking it when I hear a female voice.

"Sam!"

I look up and see a pretty woman in her 40s.

"I thought you were in Hong Kong meeting the new sales force."

"Hong Kong? . . . Oh, yes, Hong Kong. I'm afraid I missed the plane. Something came up." I wish I knew this woman's name.

I guess she thinks I'm wondering why she's working on a Saturday. She says, "I came in to catch up. You know what madness it was here yesterday!"

"You can say that again."

"You look like you've just crossed Death Valley, Sam."

"I *feel* like it," I answer, thinking I must look pretty bad. I can't remember when I last slept or washed up. Quickly I try to think of something to explain why I look so ragged.

"My car broke down, and I had to walk to get here. The shop says it won't be ready for a few days. Now I'm not sure what to do."

"What do you mean? Why don't you just rent a car?"

"What?" I ask, surprised that cars can be rented so easily. She gets a questioning look on her face. Again I try to cover myself. "I mean, who do you use?"

"The same people the company uses. . . . Listen, do you want me to call them for you?"

"That would be very kind of you. I've got a lot on my mind just now and—"

"Think nothing of it," she says, turning toward the phone on a nearby desk.

I walk into what I hope is my office. It's the largest one. I step over to the desk and see calling cards that read, "North American

Testing Services, Sam Smith, President." I sit down in the chair and listen in on one end of the phone call.

"Hello, this is Judy. Mr. Smith will be needing a car for the next few days. Could you drop one by? . . . Just put it in the company name. . . . Great. Thanks a lot. Bye."

I hear the phone being hung up. Then Judy is in my doorway.

"The car will be here within the hour. They'll leave it where they always do, in your parking spot. The keys will be under the seat."

"Thank you, Judy," I say, suddenly feeling great warmth for a woman I don't even know. My visits with Brad and Hugh are still fresh in my mind. Now I need someone to like me. Now I want this woman to tell me what a good person I am. I want her to tell me how much she enjoys working for me.

"Well, I'd better get going. I've got a dog to walk and a kitchen to clean."

"Judy?"

"Yes?"

"Are you happy working here?"

"Why . . . yes."

"Are you making enough money?"

She laughs. "Well, I can't say I didn't feel your last pay cut. But I guess I'm making ends meet all right."

"Well, the company is lucky to have you. One way or another we'll make up for that pay cut."

"Thanks, Sam. Good night."

"Good night," I say, looking at the empty doorway. I turn my heavy high-backed chair around to face the window.

It's a clear day. When I crashed, the air was thick with dust. I could hardly see a thing. Now I can see buildings in Santa Monica and the ocean behind them. The sun is starting to set. Slowly the sky above the water is changing color from light orange to deep red.

Nothing of my life or work has come back to me. I don't know the first thing about turning on a television, let alone about writing tests.

I turn and look around the room. On a table in the corner is a picture of a woman in her 50s. She has orange-red hair. *Could this be my wife?* Her hair makes me think of the woman I saw just before the crash. *Could they be one and the same?* I decide the chances are small.

I face my desk. A date book is opened to August 29, 1986. Next to 9:00 A.M. is written "board meeting." Next to 1:45 P.M. is "Carlton Breeze." *Who's that?* I ask myself. Finally, next to 3:30 P.M., is "Pan Am, flight 92."

I was supposed to go to Hong Kong. But something stopped me. Could whatever it was have anything to do with my forgetting so much of my life?

Suddenly I want only to go home.

The sun is now slipping quickly into the ocean. I start going through my desk drawers, looking for something that can tell me where I live. Soon I spot a small off-white card. It reads, "Dinner for the American Cancer Society. $500 per plate." The dinner has already taken place— on Sunday, July 27, 1986. At the bottom of the card are the words "Alice and Sam Smith, 2250 Eastgate Drive." I know the street. It's north of Sunset Boulevard. I push back my chair and start to stand, but I have a hard time moving my legs. They feel locked. I rub them, wondering, *Is this what old age is?* Finally I get to the elevator. Inside, I press "P" for what I hope is parking.

There aren't many cars, but it still takes awhile to find my spot. I walk around two whole floors before I see "Sam Smith" painted on a wall. In front of my name is a car with the

word "Chrysler" on its trunk. To the right of that are the words "New Yorker." I open the door and sit behind the wheel. My heart is pounding, my mouth is dry, and my hands are cold. I'm not looking forward to driving another one of these space-age cars. But I reach under the front seat for the keys and then start it.

Suddenly, I hear a man's voice. Quickly, I look behind me for a robber. I'm thinking that I'm a sitting duck down there by myself when I hear it again.

"Please fasten your seat belt," says the voice.

I turn off the car and look around some more. Then I realize that the voice was coming from inside the car! I begin going through the pockets in the doors for an owner's book. I find it along with a map of the city. I spend several minutes learning where things are in both the car and the city.

Chapter **6**

HOME

The parking lot is a strange dark underworld. I follow the exit signs and keep circling up. Before long, I see streetlights shining through an open door.

I inch the car forward, onto a street called Constellation Boulevard. The windows of the buildings are brightly lit against the night sky. In my mirror, I see a fountain behind me. It, too, is all lit up, and the water shooting from it is sparkling.

I've decided to take the San Diego Freeway home. It's the one they said I crashed on, which scares me. Yet I'm thinking that driving it might help me remember something. The map showed an exit off Sunset, which is what I want. I can take the San Diego Freeway to Sunset Boulevard and then be just a few minutes from Eastgate Drive.

As soon as I'm on the freeway, I want to get off of it. It was madness to think I could handle all the cars and lights crashing through the darkness around me. I stay in the far right lane and stick to 45 miles an hour. The next thing I know a sign reading "Sunset Blvd., ½ mile" flashes by. At Sunset, I get off the freeway and then pull over and stop the car. It takes me a few minutes to get control of myself. I wait for the traffic to die down. Then I pull back onto the street. I turn left on Eastgate Drive and am soon passing large rich-looking homes. Finally I see the number 2250 below a front door light.

Something tells me to check out the place before going in. I park the car a few houses down, take out my keys, and jump at the sound of a man's voice. "Your headlights are on."

The smell of summer flowers fills the air. Moonlight dances off the trees. I walk back up the street and stop at the end of the driveway to 2250.

The house is half-lit by the streetlights. It's a long one-story building made of river rock and redwood. The windows are dark but for one light burning at the far end. I move toward the backyard. There I see a swimming pool and a large greenhouse.

Finally I force myself to look into the house. Inside, the same woman in the picture in my office is talking on the phone. I hear her voice pretty clearly, even through the closed window. She's saying, "Yes, Carlton, I know you asked me not to call until things blow over. . . . Yes, I got the office set up in San Francisco. I flew

back today. Carlton, I need to know what happened! Sam never got on the plane!

"I went to where he said he'd leave me the car and it wasn't there. Then I checked with Pan Am. They say he never boarded. I just got home now. His bags are still here on the bed, along with his passport! Where is he, Carlton? . . . That's great, just great. Now listen, we've got to think this thing out. I'm coming over to your office right now. . . . Well, what time *would* be good? . . . Okay, I'll meet you there in an hour. That'll give me time to check his office. I'll see you at nine. Don't keep me waiting, Carlton."

I don't know what to make of all this. Is she worried about me or about something else? My guess is that the Carlton she's just called is the Carlton I supposedly saw yesterday. Is he a friend of ours? I think about going inside and showing myself but decide against it. Something tells me this woman doesn't have my best interests in mind.

I stay out of sight until I hear her lock the front door. I then watch her get into her car and race down the driveway. The next few minutes I spend looking for an open window. Suddenly I hear footsteps behind me.

"Hands up!" a voice shouts.

I turn around and see a tall man pointing a gun at me.

"Oh, Sam, it's only you—I'm sorry. I was watching from my bedroom window. I thought you were a robber about to break in. But what are you doing here, anyway? You're supposed to be in Hong Kong."

"Oh, you know how it goes," I say, wishing I knew the man's name. "Some last-minute business came up. . . . Say, I've got a little problem here. I left my keys at the office. In fact, I *was* just getting ready to break in."

"Don't do that. I've got a set of keys to your house." The man reaches into his pocket and hands me the keys. "Alice asked me to check on things while you were both out of town."

"I should have checked with you first," I say, taking the keys. "Thanks for keeping an eye on the house."

"Hey, what are neighbors for?"

I walk past the pool and open the back door. In the kitchen, I suddenly realize I haven't eaten all day. I open the icebox and grab a leftover chicken breast. Everything but the glass table is black. On the table is a cleaner's bag of clothes. I read a note tied to the hangers. It says, "Mr. Smith, Sorry we were late and missed you." I finish eating and clean up. Then I walk through the all-white living room, past a wall of river rock. There are two bedrooms. I find a suitcase in one of them. Resting on top of it is my passport, with my picture in it. It says I was born in L.A. in 1924. From its pages drops a New York driver's license. My name is on the license. *There's something not right here,* I think.

I walk into the study. Its walls are lined with hundreds of books. From a table, I pick up a book of pictures. The first page shows Alice and me on the day we got married. Looking closely I realize that Alice *is* the same woman I saw before the crash. As I turn the pages I see us becoming older and better off. By the end of the book, we've traveled all over the world. I've seen no children.

I step over to the desk. There's a small machine of some kind sitting in the center of it. I press a button marked "On" and hear a man's voice. The man is talking very slowly. He's saying, "Now, close your eyes. Think peaceful thoughts. . . . Find a spot in your mind where no one can reach you. . . ."

Suddenly, I realize that the machine must record voices. I've never seen anything like it. Then I realize that the man talking is hypnotizing someone.

". . . You have no worries. You are feeling free, very free. You—"

I press a button marked "Fast Forward" and lift my finger. Now the voice is saying, "I used to smoke, but now that's something I don't do anymore." *This man is trying to help someone to stop smoking,* I think. I press "Stop," the top pops up, and I look inside at a small thin box. On it are the words Open Eye, Inc. Below them is the name Carlton Breeze, along with his place of business, in Century City. Written in the corner is a note: "Sam, play three times every day."

Me? Smoke? When did I start smoking? And why haven't I wanted a cigarette all day?

That must be why I was seeing Carlton at 1:45 yesterday. Or was it?

I check my watch and see I've got just enough time to make it to Century City by 9:00. I want to be there for Alice's meeting with Carlton. I take the recording machine with me.

CHAPTER 7

MISSING PIECES

Open Eye, Inc., are the words below the number 611 on Carlton Breeze's office door. I open it a crack, hear no voices, and step inside. I find myself in a waiting room with two chairs, a lamp, and nothing to read. Before me is another door. From behind it come the voices of Alice and the man on the machine.

ALICE: I know you've ordered people to do things against their wills before. I know we're onto something that will change the study of the human mind forever. But it looks like this time it didn't work. Sam never went to the bank.

CARLTON: How do you know?

ALICE: I called from San Francisco just before they closed. . . . What a mess! We don't even know where he is! He didn't go to the bank.

He didn't go to Hong Kong. Maybe he's on to us.

CARLTON: I don't think so, Alice. As of 3:35 yesterday, he doesn't even know who you are.

ALICE: If your first order didn't work, what makes you think your second one did?

CARLTON: Something outside my control stopped him from going to the bank. Nothing could stop him from forgetting you at 3:35 yesterday.

ALICE: I wouldn't sit there smiling if I were you. We're in trouble. He's wandering around somewhere in this city. . . . How could things go so wrong? . . . Let's start at the beginning. He came to your office yesterday at 1:45 for help with his smoking, right?

CARLTON: That's right, Alice. Everything went as planned.

ALICE: You put him under?

CARLTON: I put him under and gave him his orders and—

ALICE: Stop. Tell me how you worded them.

CARLTON: This is what I said Alice, word for word. "You have a 3:30 plane to catch this afternoon. Just before driving to the airport, you will go to your bank. There, you will put your savings in your wife's name. Then you'll go to the airport and get on the plane. And at 3:35, you'll forget your wife ever lived. *You will forget everything from the minute you met her.* You will also forget these orders."

ALICE: So why didn't he go to the bank?

CARLTON: If his bags were at home, as you say, he probably headed there first.

ALICE: Of course! What time did he leave your office?

CARLTON: A little after 2:00.

ALICE: When I got home tonight, I took in a bag of clothes from the cleaners. It'd been hanging on the back door. They probably left it there yesterday. There was a note saying they were late. The clean clothes should have been brought to the house before Sam left for work. But they weren't. And that's why Sam didn't take his suitcase to the office. He knew he'd have to go back to the house for the cleaning. But he never made it back to the house.

CARLTON: Remember what you told me when we were putting this plan together? "Sam *always* takes his bags to the office and leaves from there on business trips." How was I to know he didn't have his bags? How was I to know he wasn't going back to his office? I may control minds, Alice, but I can't read them.

ALICE: So he left your office a little after 2:00. He didn't go to the bank, because *you* told him to do that later. You told him to go to the bank *just before* driving to the airport. He left your office and drove *home—away* from the bank, and *away* from the airport! He was probably on the San Diego Freeway, heading north, at about 2:30. . . . If he smashed up our new Mustang speeding, I'll kill him.

CARLTON: Wait a minute. There was an oil spill on the San Diego Freeway yesterday. Cars were held up for hours. It was a mess. Everyone was trying to get out of town for Labor Day. It was still a mess when I got on it at 4:00.

ALICE: That's great, Carlton. Sam never went to the bank, and he never went to the airport. At 3:35, when he forgot I ever lived, he was still driving on the San Diego Freeway. . . . This was going to be so easy, you said. We'd get Sam to give me his money. I'd put it into Open Eye. He'd get lost in Hong Kong and never be seen again. It was going to be a clean job, you said!

CARLTON: I think you should just do as we planned. His office will be closed Monday for Labor Day. Call in Tuesday. Sound worried. Say he never checked into the Hong Kong Hilton.

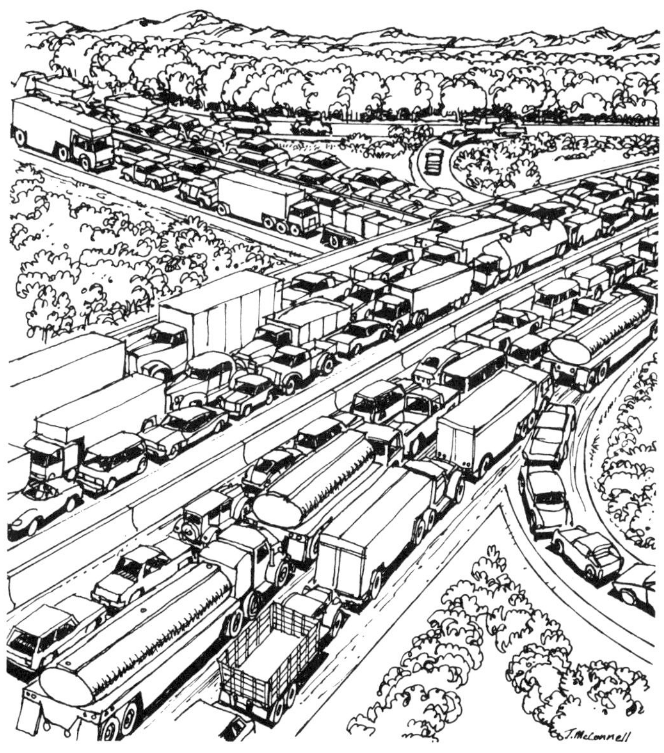

ALICE: They'll think it strange if I don't call the police. And sooner or later someone in his office will call Pan Am. Then they'll find out he never got on the plane.

CARLTON: So he's decided to drop out. He's left you *and* his business to start a new life. He's a missing person.

ALICE: He's well known in this city. The police will post his picture. Sooner or later, someone will spot him in a crowd. . . . And how will I explain the New York driver's license we got made up for him?

CARLTON: You don't know a thing about it. Listen, people will know he's not in his right mind. You'll have him put away. And *then* you can get him to sign over his money. We'll put it in our business. And that will be the end of it.

ALICE: All I want is to have what's mine, Carlton. I helped Sam make his money. He owns 19 buildings on Wilshire Boulevard thanks to me. And he makes me beg for every penny. To be done with him is more than I can hope for.

CARLTON: It would have been easier if we'd killed him, like I wanted us to do.

ALICE: Oh, you know I wouldn't kill anyone, not even Sam.

I can't listen to any more of this. I leave Carlton Breeze's office and go back to my rented car. Finally the pieces are falling together. I married a woman who got herself tied up with some crackpot hypnotist. Together they'd planned to take my money and do away with me.

The cleaners' slipup probably saved my life. If it hadn't been for that, I'd have made the bank—and the plane. I'd be in Hong Kong now, with half a memory and a New York I.D.

I decide to spend the night on the floor of my Century City office. Hours pass before I get to sleep. I'm filled with anger at this woman who calls herself my wife. I think about turning both her and Breeze over to the police.

More than anything else, I want my memory back. Breeze holds the key to it. And Alice holds the key to Breeze.

CHAPTER 8

Lost And Found

The early-morning sun wakes me up. The first thing I do is call Alice. She sounds surprised to hear my voice. I say I want to meet her and Breeze right away. She tells me to be at his Century City office at 7:00.

I open the door to Breeze's office and find both Breeze and Alice already seated. Breeze is behind his desk and Alice is to his right. "Hello, Alice," I say. I still don't recognize her as the woman I've been married to all these years.

"Hello, Sam," she answers weakly. Like Breeze, she looks pretty unhappy.

I take a seat across from Breeze, realizing my life is in his hands. I don't say much, but I do take out the recording machine. I'd brought it with me from the house last night when I came over here. When I heard Alice and Breeze going over their plans, I'd simply pressed "Record."

Now, I place the machine on Breeze's desk and press "On."

"This is what I said, Alice, word for word. 'You have a 3:30 plane to catch. . . .'"

As Breeze's voice plays, I keep my eyes on him. He looks worried. His arm begins moving below his desk. Suddenly, Breeze is pointing a gun at me.

"Carlton, no!" Alice shouts.

"Now's my chance to do what I wanted to do all along," he says.

"I wouldn't shoot if I were you," I answer, turning off the recorder. "You see, I left a copy of this at my office, along with a note. It says if I don't show up Tuesday morning, they're to call the police."

By now, Breeze is looking *very* worried. I go on talking. "I want my memory back. Give it to me now, and I won't go to the police."

As I left Breeze's office building, I reached into an empty pocket for a cigarette. It was then that I realized I had 42 years of memory back. I also had back the habit I'd started just after leaving school. I looked at the buildings around me. Finally I could remember them.

Finally I could remember my life. I sat down on a stone wall as the memories washed over me. They came in no clear order.

I remembered my parents getting killed in the plane crash. I remembered being married to Alice. I remembered our fights over money. I remembered my falling out with Brad and then with Hugh. I remembered coming here to Century City every day for work. I remembered Alice telling me about this wonderful hypnotist she'd met. I'd been seeing him every Friday at 1:45. He was going to help me stop smoking. I remembered my plans to leave for Hong Kong on Friday. I remembered smashing up our new Mustang on the way home for my bags.

I even remembered the first time I'd seen Alice. It was 1944. Her Ford had a flat. I pulled over and changed her tire. She was the most beautiful woman I'd ever seen.

Where had we gone wrong? When had money become more important to us than each other? That I couldn't remember yet.

I looked up at the sky. It was as blue as it gets in L.A. The streets of Century City were empty. I could even hear a few birds.

I thought again about turning Alice and Breeze over to the police. But I wasn't sure the

police would believe me—even with the recording. (Of course, I was happy that Breeze was afraid they would.) Besides, I didn't want to go back on my word not to turn them in. I felt that one way or another I'd hurt enough people for a lifetime.

I looked down the street. The Century Plaza Hotel was sparkling in the mid-morning sun.

Water from the fountain in front of it was splashing on the ground. I watched an airplane move slowly across the sky. I looked at my watch. It was eight o'clock. *At this time yesterday*, I thought, *I was in the hospital.*

I'd been living a bad dream for 24 hours. It felt like a lifetime.

I walked over to the hotel and got myself a room. It was there that I realized what I had to do.

I pulled up in front of Brad's house and saw him at his gardening. When I closed my car door, Brad looked up. Then his mouth dropped open. I guess he couldn't believe I'd come back after all he'd said to me yesterday.

"I've done a lot of thinking over the past 24 hours, Brad. I'm sorry that I've lost you as a friend."

I handed Brad a check for $26,400.00.

"I know this won't buy you back. But I want you to have it anyway. It's your half of the money I made on the Catalina house."

Brad took the check in his dirt-covered hands. I turned and walked to my car.

Minutes later, I found Hugh in his backyard, cutting the grass.

"I spent all of Saturday night at my office, Hugh. I was going over our records. The company is growing faster than I can handle. What we need is a man who's good with numbers. We've got money in too many different places. I need someone to keep track of it."

Hugh's eyes followed a bird shooting across the sky. "You should get yourself a young man, someone fresh out of school."

"Young people don't know anything about company loyalty," I said. "I want someone who's going to stick around. . . . I was thinking that someone might be you."

"What changed your mind?" Hugh asked, looking me in the eye.

"That's a long story," I answered.

We both smiled.

"Well, Sam, I guess I can still add two and two," Hugh said. "I suppose I could give you some help on the numbers end of your business. Let me talk it over with my wife. I'll get back to you in the next day or so."

"Please do that," I said, shaking his hand.

Hugh walked me back to my car. Already, the light was returning to his eyes. They'd seemed half-dead the day before. I, too, was beginning to feel better than I had in a long, long time.

As I pulled away from Hugh's house, I waved out the window to him. Hugh waved back. Somehow I knew his decision was already made.

Finally, I turned onto the street where I used to live. I knocked on the door of the house my father had built. The woman I met yesterday morning opened it. She took one look at me and said, "You've come for the box. It's right here, Mr. Smith."

She left the doorway and in a second was back with my belongings. Taking them from her, I said, "Thanks for holding on to these things." Walking to my car, I thought, *I'll hold on to them for the rest of my days.*

Three months passed. Hugh and I were at the office early. We were going over sales records before our board meeting later that day. We were rushing through them because we were meeting Brad for breakfast at 8:00. At the same time, I was looking at the headlines in the *L.A. Times.* Hugh was reading out the numbers for September when my eye caught the following.

HYPNOTIST INDICTED FOR FRAUD

Century City hypnotist Carlton Breeze has been indicted for making false business claims. Mr. Breeze is founder and president of Open Eye, Inc. He will appear before a grand jury on December 16.

Also named in the indictment was Alice Smith, Vice President of the company. Mr. Breeze and Ms. Smith were released on bail Thursday.

Both Breeze and Smith refused to answer questions. However, one patient was willing to talk as long as his name would not be used. The young man said, "They started telling me they could change my life forever. They said they could make me do, say, think, or forget anything! I got scared. Man, all I wanted was to stop biting my fingernails."

Open Eye's home office is in Century City. However, new offices were opened in San Francisco last September. And plans were in the works for adding offices throughout the country. Undercover agents say they have been watching the business closely for several months.

I thought about Open Eye's claims and about what had happened to me last summer. And I was grateful. If Breeze and Alice hadn't tried to get me lost, I might never have found myself.